Beautiful America's

Seattle

Front cover: A beautiful day in Seattle

Published by
Beautiful America Publishing Company
P.O. Box 244
Woodburn, OR 97071

Library of Congress Catalog Number 89-17800

ISBN 0-89802-708-X
ISBN 0-89802-707-1 (paperback)

Copyright 1999 by Beautiful America Publishing Company ©

Fireworks display over Seattle

Beautiful America's
Seattle

By Cheryl Landes

Photography by Terry Donnelly

Beautiful America Publishing Company

Contents

Introduction

As an outdoor enthusiast, I have never been fond of large cities. These concrete jungles were places where I attended conferences and meetings or shopped for items not easily found in the small town where I lived. Cities were too congested with people and cars, had streets darkened from towering skyscrapers, and didn't have enough trees. There were no hiking trails, and riding a bicycle was impossible.

My impressions changed during my first visit to Seattle. The sweeping views of ferries gliding effortlessly across Puget Sound with the rugged snow-capped Olympic Mountains on the horizon, the lush greenery, the salt breeze, and the skyscrapers' lights reflecting in the water at night reeled me in. Less than a year later I moved here and have lived here ever since. That was 10 years ago.

Today, Seattle still retains its friendly, welcoming, small-town persona despite a population exceeding 2.7 million. And although it has been around for more than a century, it manages to fuel the youthful creativity of a host of talented writers, artists, musicians, inventors, and software developers. It's the birthplace of grunge rock, the espresso coffee craze, and Heart, the Wilson sisters' rock band. It's also the home of the late rock guitarist Jimi Hendrix, saxophonist Kenny G., Mariners' centerfielder Ken Griffey, Jr., glass artist Dave Chihuly, actor Tom Skerritt, Microsoft co-founder Bill Gates, and grunge bands Pearl Jam and Soundgarden.

The climate is mild year-round, the result of the city's proximity to the sea. Summer temperatures rarely creep above the high 70s/low 80s and stay mostly in the low to high 40s in the winter. Rain seems to be a constant companion from October through May. Although the rain gauges average 36 inches a year – less than the annual rainfall for Atlanta and New York – it falls much lighter and

City skyline and the Bell Street Harbor Marina

Opposite page: Skyline at dusk

slower than in other places in the country. We have several words for rain, just like the Eskimos have 12 words for snow.

Speaking of snow, it's rare. Usually we'll have a dusting in November or December and will see no more flakes until the following winter. Occasionally, though, when the rain systems from the southwest and the cold fronts from Alaska or British Columbia's Fraser Valley collide, much larger accumulations are possible. Eight inches blanketed the city in the winter of 1990. Six years later on the day after Christmas, 2 feet fell within four hours. It was the worst storm in 30 years, according to weather forecasters and old-timers. The snow seldom lasts beyond one or two days, because rain riding the coat tails of a warm front washes it away.

In November 1851, the schooner *Exact* deposited the first white families on Alki Point. The Arthur Denny party, which consisted of 10 adults and 12 children, built some crude cabins on Alki Beach. After battling a winter of fierce wind and rain storms, they moved the town east next to the protected waters of Elliott Bay. They named the city Seattle after Chief Sealth, the leader of the Duwamish and Suquamish tribes who helped the party survive.

The fledging metropolis grew rapidly, attracting lumberjacks, traders, fur trappers, and missionaries. The city grew even faster during the Klondike Gold Rush, when Seattle became known as the jumping off point to the gold fields of the Yukon. Between 1890 and 1910, the population increased sixfold. Tideflats along the present Waterfront area and south of Pioneer Square were filled in and the steep hills in the Denny Regrade area were leveled. Since then, the economy has had its ups and downs, but remains strong. Boeing, the only airplane manufacturer in the United States, is still the largest employer. One hundred thousand people build jets and defense aircraft in plants scattered from Everett to Renton. The Red Barn, Boeing's first manufacturing plant, is now part of the Museum of Flight, and the Everett plant gives visitors tours for a small fee.

Today, high-tech is the rising star in Seattle's industrial scene. The Puget Sound area is now known as the "Silicon Forest" because of the swift growth of software, medical, and telecommunications companies. Microsoft, founded in 1975, has mushroomed to a miniature city of sorts within Redmond. Smaller companies, such as Adobe, Attachmate, Visio, and WRQ, have solid shares in their market niches.

Through it all, the attraction to the Alki Beach never faded. Today, it attracts sunbathers, volleyball players, and couples enjoying the sweeping panoramas of the sound, mountains, and skyscrapers. A constant stream of joggers, walkers, roller skaters, and bikers follow the paved trail running parallel to the beach, and at night, bonfires light the sky. A miniature Statue of Liberty marks the site where the Denny party landed almost 150 years ago.

Downtown Seattle

Few downtowns compare with Seattle for its diversity. Many of us locals describe life in Seattle with the old cliché, "having the best of both worlds." Downtown Seattle, it seems to me, has a split personality. Although it's a bustling mix of office and retail, it hasn't lost touch with its natural side. One minute you're engrossed in the glamour of the gleaming skyscrapers and shopping at top-name retailers; the next, you're on a street corner savoring a sweeping panorama of Elliott Bay and the Olympic Mountains while waiting for the signal to change from "Don't Walk" to "Walk."

In the midst of its modern architecture and splendid natural beauty, downtown Seattle hasn't forgotten its heritage. Blocks of brick buildings dating back to 1889 – the year Washington became a state – are still standing in the Pioneer Square National Historic District. The buildings in this 20-square-block area have been lovingly restored and are now filled with gift and souvenir shops, bookstores, toy stores, cafés, and art galleries that attract thousands of tourists and local shoppers every year. Fountains of petunias and geraniums overflow window boxes and pots hanging from lampposts. Grand shade trees aged 50 years or more are also common fixtures of the district as are the brick walkways. Younger trees, daffodils, and other perennials thrive in the soil of the traffic medians. And when you tire of walking, you can hire a horse-drawn carriage to give you a tour of the district and the neighboring Waterfront.

Not only is history above ground, but it's also underground. That's because originally, the Pioneer Square district was much lower than it is today. Before 1889, the year the city was devastated by the Great Seattle Fire (which started when a painter's glue pot boiled over) the streets were at ground level. Backed-up sewage and muddy, often impassable, streets were constant problems, because most of the square was at or below sea level. From 1891 to 1905, the streets were elevated to the second story – from 8 to 35 feet – on wood, brick, or stone trestles. Soon the ground-level businesses were abandoned and covered at the second story.

You can relive this hidden Seattle today by taking the Underground Tour 360 days a year. It begins at Doc Maynard's Public House (named for one of the city's original founders with a reputation for his vision and his love of the grape), where guides provide a lively 20-minute history of early Seattle and its founders. From there, the tour continues underground to three old businesses: the Scandinavian American Bank, where you'll walk through the former safe; the Merchants Store, a mercantile; and the Bijou Theater. Much of the original pressed tin ceiling is still intact at the Bijou. The tour ends at a small museum in the basement of the Howard building, which is filled with photographs, drawings, and newspaper clippings of Seattle's early history.

More history thrives in one of the few indoor national parks in the country – the Klondike Gold Rush National Park, across the street from Occidental Park. The park, actually more like a museum, is packed with displays that show how the discovery of gold in Dawson City, Yukon, affected Seattle's economy at the turn of the century. Thanks to some quick thinking by a local promoter, Seattle became the "jumping-off point" for potential prospectors dreaming of endless wealth. They stopped here on the way north to buy the ton of food, clothing, and equipment the Northwest Canadian Mounted Police required each person to carry into the Yukon because supplies ran short there during the long, cold winters. Then they booked passage on anything that floated – literally – to make the long journey to Alaska, where they would hike across rocky terrain and treacherous mountains to reach the Klondike. For many who made the long journey, their dreams were never realized. By the time they arrived, all of the best claims had been staked. Those who stayed worked for other miners or started their own businesses.

Elliott Bay Marina and city skyline

Seattle at dusk

Inside the park, you'll find dramatic pictures of stampeders carrying supplies up the Chilkoot Trail in Alaska, one of the main routes to the goldfields; lucky prospectors holding pans filled with gold; and a floor-to-ceiling photograph of the *SS Portland*, which broke the news of the gold rush when it arrived in Seattle with a ton of gold and some 60 miners from Dawson City in July 1897. Other displays include goods sold in Seattle during the Klondike Gold Rush and old newspaper articles. More information about the gold rush and its effects on Seattle is provided in four 25-minute slide shows.

Pioneer Square was the birthplace of the original "Skid Road," Yesler Way. In the early days, when logging was one of the fledgling city's major industries, timber was slid down the steep muddy grade to Henry Yesler's steam-powered mill on the Waterfront. The nickname evolved into "skid row," which refers to the thousands of homeless people inhabiting any major city.

Pioneer Square is also a people-watcher's paradise. Grab a sandwich, a cup of Joe, and a cookie at one of the assorted delis and dine on the benches, or hang out at a sidewalk café. Often, the local inhabitants are more interesting to observe than the tourists.

The district is well known for two events. The first, the Fat Tuesday Celebration, happens just before Lent begins. The most popular activity during this wild affair is a Spam carving contest, where aspiring sculptors empty dozens of cans of the processed meat and let their creative juices flow. Creations have ranged from animals to abstract art.

Art is the focus of the other event, a weekly art walk on the first Thursday evening of the month, which loops through the galleries of Pioneer Square, the Pike Place Market area, and the Seattle Art Museum (SAM). SAM and its sister, the Asian Art Museum in Volunteer Park, stay open late on those nights, and admission is free. Outside SAM, the four-story black sculpture "Hammering Man" stands guard at the entrance. Inside, the grand marble stairway, guarded at the base by two marble lions, leads to permanent exhibits of African and

Space Needle and boats of Lake Union at night

Northwest Indian art, contemporary painting and sculptures, and traveling exhibits from around the world. Past special exhibits included Leonardo da Vinci's original manuscripts (owned by Microsoft co-founder Bill Gates), Egyptian artifacts, and the paintings of the late Thomas Moran, who is famous for his images of Yellowstone National Park. A small café inside the museum serves cold gourmet entrees, soup, and rich desserts. The bowl of salmon chowder and a roll is a meal in itself, not to mention one of my favorite lunches downtown.

Food – lots of it – can be found at the oldest continually operating open-air market in the country one block north of SAM. Pike Place Market is like a daily Saturday Market, only much bigger. Upon first glance, the old wooden beams, creaky floors, and tall pillars that support the maze of stalls give the market an unsteady appearance, but it's structurally sound. The market is an institution in Seattle; many of the merchants have had stalls there for more than 50 years. Fresh fruits and vegetables, trucked in each morning from farmlands north and south of the city, abound in the Farmer's Market on the upper level. Other merchants peddle tea and coffee, spices, and cheese, along with handmade jewelry, wind-up toys, clothing, pottery, and paper crafts. My favorite shop is Read All About It at the market's main entrance, which sells newspapers and magazines from practically everywhere in the world.

If you're from out of town, stop by the Pike Place Fish Market for some fresh seafood and have it shipped directly to your house. The antics and one-liners of the workers selecting and packaging fish are one of the best free comedy acts around. Strolling musicians, mimes, and magicians contribute to the market's festive flavor.

If you don't want to cook, you'll also find prepared food selections as vast as the Pacific Ocean at the market. Cafés and restaurants serve homemade pastries, salads, sandwiches, microbrews, wine, and a variety of gourmet dishes. There's also the original Starbucks, which, more than two decades ago, started the latté craze in Seattle that has now spread to the East Coast. The frenzy hasn't left Seattle, either. Almost anywhere you go downtown, there's a Starbucks, Tully's, SBC (Seattle's Best Coffee), or mom-and-pop espresso cart on virtually every block.

One of the most recent additions to the market is the Giant Shoe Museum. Dan Eskenazi, a Seattle native who has collected oversized footwear for more than 30 years, opened the coin-operated museum in the lower level of the market in 1997. Among the assortment of large shoes are a 5-foot-long black wingtip, a 2-foot-6-inch-tall Army boot dating from the Vietnam War, and a size 37AA black high-top oxford that was believed to be worn by the world's tallest man, Robert Wadlow of Illinois.

Behind the market is the Waterfront with an assortment of antique and gift shops and more places to eat. My favorite shop there is Ye Old Curiosity Shop at Pier 54, which has an interesting mix of gaudy souvenirs, ranging from miniature totem poles to hot pink plastic back scratchers, and offbeat displays. The strangest exhibit is a shrunken head. Harbor tours depart next door. At the Seattle Aquarium on Pier 59, view the collection of thousands of species of marine life, including fishes, eels, octopi, and a pair of playful otters. The adjoining Omnidome shows a number of nature films, ranging from a documentary on whales to exploring the Grand Canyon, along with its ongoing feature, "The Eruption of Mount St. Helens." The latter takes you on an airplane ride into the dome of the erupting crater in 1980. In July and August, you can enjoy the sunset while listening to the music of top performers, such as Joan Baez, Chris Isaak, and k.d. lang, at Waterfront Park.

Ivar's Acres of Clams at Pier 54 is another local institution. Here at the snack bar, the late Ivar Haglund began his restaurant empire, where you can still buy fish and chips made from his original recipe or clam chowder. Gourmet seafood selections can be had in his restaurant behind the snack bar.

When Ivar died, he left a gift to Seattle's citizens – funding for the spectacular

Seattle from First Hill

Opposite page: Freeway Park and Convention Center

Path to Tribe Street ↗

annual fireworks display over Elliott Bay on the Fourth of July. Another dazzling Independence Day display is sponsored by AT&T over Lake Union, where spectators crowd Gasworks Park as early as sunrise with picnic baskets and blankets to stake out that perfect spot to gaze upon the giant sparklers.

Myrtle Edwards Park, next to the Edgewater Hotel, is the popular viewing site for the fireworks over Elliott Bay. But on other days of the year, it's a popular spot for short walks and picnics. A sweeping view of the Olympic Mountains, Mount Rainier, and the ferries crossing Puget Sound is the main attraction. The green and white ferries shaped like wedding cakes depart from Coleman Dock (Pier 52) to Bremerton and Bainbridge Island on the Olympic Peninsula, and Vashon Island between West Seattle and the peninsula.

Bird's-eye views can be found at three spots downtown. At the top of the 42-story Smith Tower, Seattle's first skyscraper built in 1914 near Occidental Park, you'll see the grand historical district, Elliott Bay, and the Olympics from the observation deck. Built by the founder of the Smith-Corona Typewriter Company, the tower was at one time the highest west of the Mississippi River. When another building outside the state threatened this dubious distinction, he erected a flagpole at the top.

Today, Smith Tower is a dwarf in comparison to the Columbia Center, a 76-story black glass skyscraper that now holds the honor of the tallest building west of the Mississippi. Many Seattleites affectionately call it the "Darth Vader Building" because of its ominous appearance. You can take a series of elevators to the 72nd floor for a 270-degree view of the metro area, where on clear days, you can see as far south as Sea-Tac International Airport and beyond the Space Needle.

At the Seattle Center, the site of the 1962 World's Fair, you'll feel on top of the world at the 605-foot Space Needle, the city's most popular landmark and the youngest structure designated a National Historic Landmark. Take the 43-second elevator ride to the observation platform at the 520-foot level and soak in the 360-

degree panorama, or dine in the rotating restaurant below. The restaurant makes one complete circle every 58 minutes and serves exquisite Northwest cuisine. Be forewarned – the restaurant is very expensive but well worth it for the quality of the food, service, and the view. (The cost for a couple, including drinks and dessert, exceeds $100.) Clear days reveal rare views of Mount Baker, just south of the Canadian border, and the Cascade Mountains to the east of Seattle.

The 74-acre complex is also the site of the Pacific Science Center and the Key Arena, the home of the Supersonics basketball franchise and Thunderbirds minor-league hockey team. Children can explore the Children's Museum or take carnival rides in the Fun Forest Amusement Park. Three major events are held at the center every year: Northwest Folklife Festival, featuring art and music on Memorial Day weekend; The Bite in July, where you'll find some of the best strawberry shortcake around; and Bumbershoot, supposedly named to appease the rain gods. This festival on Labor Day weekend features live music, dance, theater, film, comedy, artists, writers, an International Bazaar, and the Taste of Seattle. The Seattle Children's Theater, the Seattle Repertory Theater, and the Intiman Theater Company entertain audiences year-round.

Hop aboard the Monorail for a one-minute ride from the Seattle Center to a shopper's paradise along Fourth, Fifth, and Sixth Avenues. Here, you'll find such well-known retailers as FAO Schwartz, Eddie Bauer, Niketown, Levi Strauss, Nordstrom, Talbots, and Old Navy. Westlake Center, the stop for the Monorail, and Pacific Place are filled with more shops, ranging from Tiffany's in the latter to Brentano's in the former. There's even a Planet Hollywood, where famous TV and movie star sightings have been common, especially when film crews are in town.

Nearby on Third Avenue between University and Union Streets, Benaroya Hall features regular performances by the Seattle Symphony Orchestra and concerts by well-known musicians, such as jazz pianist Jim Brickman. The symphony hall, which opened in the fall of 1998, boasts the best acoustics of any

Garden fountain and walkway

The city from Kerry Park

concert facility in the nation, and the custom glass sculptures, blown locally, are magnificent.

The International District, which borders Pioneer Square on the east, has a reputation for some of the best Asian food in Seattle. Its Chinatown, one of the largest in America, features restaurants ranging from small family-style spots to larger establishments ornately decorated in black, red, and gold—all reasonably priced. There are also equally fine Korean, Philippino, Thai, and Vietnamese restaurants. Hing Hay and Kobe Parks are worth a stop, as well as the Wing Luke Asian Museum. Named after Wing Luke, the son of an immigrant laundryman and Seattle's first Asian city councilman, it is the only pan-Asian museum in the United States. The permanent exhibit tells the story of how Asians and Pacific Islanders immigrated to and settled in Washington throughout the last 200 years. Uwajimaya, Inc., an authentic Japanese supermarket with exotic foods, toys, and dishes, is another permanent fixture. My favorite items there are the wide assortment of bottled sauces used for stir fry, especially the Jade Peanut Sauce.

Construction never seems to end in downtown Seattle. In the decade I've lived here, I can't recall a time when I haven't seen at least one crane in the skyline. During the late-1980s to mid-1990s, office towers consisted of most of the new real estate; now it's mostly high-rise apartments, condos, and hotels. One of the newest hotels, the Monaco, will loan guests goldfish when they're feeling lonely. Other hotels range from the European-style Alexis and Sorrento, the Old World elegance of the Four Seasons Olympic, to the standard national hotel chains: Hilton, Sheraton, Marriott, Stouffer Madison, and Ramada. Rooms fill up quickly, fueled by a constant array of conferences, meetings, and shows in the Washington State Convention Center with its 371,000 square feet of space stretching above Interstate 5, and smaller conference centers scattered throughout the city.

Soon the Kingdome, Seattle's second best-known landmark, will be a distant memory. The white orange-juicer shaped stadium that has been a part of the skyline for some 20 years is in its last season of hosting the Mariners and the Seahawks. By the time these words appear in print, baseball fans will be watching the Mariners play outdoors in Safeco Field. On rainy days, a retractable roof will keep players and spectators dry. Once the dust settles from the Kingdome's implosion next March, a new outdoor football stadium for the Seahawks will rise from the rubble.

Lake Union Dry Dock

Opposite page: Shilshole Bay Marina

Waterways

In the last edition of this book, author Anne Rule wrote, "Seattle is a 'Scorpio City' – based on the month she was founded, but she might better be a Pisces." Water is truly everywhere. Practically anywhere you go, there's a view of the sound, lakes, the ship canal, rivers, and streams. Seagulls glide effortlessly on the breezes, and the smell of salt fills the air, even during high tide.

Water drives a major portion of Seattle's economy – shipping. Container ships from Asia anchor in Elliott Bay to wait their turn to be unloaded and loaded by the giant red cranes lining the edges of the terminals on Harbor Island, one of the city's major industrial areas. Tugs assist ships in and out of the docks, and tow barges across the sound to Tacoma and the oil terminals in Anacortes and Alaska.

For the residents, the local bodies of water are as much a part of their lives as the rain, so much that I'd venture to say it's the main source of recreation. (After all, we do own more boats per capita than any other place in America!) On the first day of boating season in May, hundreds of sailboats, yachts, motorboats, kayaks, and canoes converge on Lake Union, Lake Washington, and Puget Sound and continue throughout the fall. Some hardy souls won't let the chill of winter stop them from enjoying this, their favorite pastime.

Lake Washington, the largest in the area, is the dividing line between Seattle proper and the "Eastside" – the smaller towns of Bellevue, Kirkland, Redmond, Woodinville, Duvall, Carnation, Issaquah, Fall City, and North Bend. Once bedroom communities, these neighbors have experienced growing pains from the influx of high-tech companies in Redmond and Bellevue, as well as the booming economy in general. Ten years ago, if your schedule was flexible, you could avoid the rush hour across the Mercer Island and Evergreen Point floating bridges – the two main routes from east to west – by waiting for Eastsiders to settle into their jobs in Seattle in the morning and into their homes in the evening. No longer. Now, Seattleites commute east in volumes as large as travelers westward, resulting in traffic jams in both directions.

No matter which way you're going, though, the drive is a scenic treat, especially on clear days. The snowy cap of Mount Rainier dominates the backdrop at the south end of Lake Washington, a gleaming sapphire sprinkled with milky-white sailboats and water skiers. You might even catch a faint glimpse of Mount Baker, Washington's tallest mountain, just south of the Canadian border. On stormy days, winds often churn the lake into waves high enough to break over the floating bridges.

Lake Washington is also the home of the annual hydroplane races in early August – the grand finale of Seattle's month-long summer festival, Seafair. More than 100,000 spectators pack the benches at 277-acre Seward Park or dock their boats at the log jams along the race course to watch the hydros send giant "rooster-tails" of backwash above the lake at speeds far exceeding 100 miles an hour.

Lake Union was originally landlocked, but the construction of the ship canal changed that. High-rise apartments, condos, and hotels surround the lake on three sides; Gasworks Park, the city's most popular kite-flying spot, resides on the north shore. Seaplanes land and depart for the San Juan Islands and British Columbia as tour boats and sailboats cruise by. The lake is best known for its tight-knit houseboat community along Eastlake and Westlake Avenues, where long wooden walkways stretch to docks lined with the floating homes. Flowers brighten the docks; colorful banners flap in the gentle breezes; sailboats, canoes, and kayaks replace cars outside the front doors. Many of the older wooden structures have given way to large, multi-million dollar models resembling the houseboat Tom Hanks occupied in the movie, "Sleepless in Seattle." More houseboats are scattered along the shoreline where Montlake Cut, the eastern end of the ship canal, connects Lake Union to Lake Washington.

A short distance north next to Aurora Avenue, walkers, joggers, in-line skaters, and bikers manage to circle the 3-mile paved trail around Green Lake without any mishaps. Ducks, geese, and water lilies thrive here, and occasionally bald eagles perch in the trees of the island at the north end of the lake. An annual milk carton derby, where contestants try to stay afloat in "vessels" built from milk cartons, attracts large crowds.

The Hiram M. Chittenden Locks, also known as the Ballard Locks, are among the busiest in the Americas. On sunny days and holiday weekends, commercial and pleasure boats rock like toys in a bathtub as they're hoisted from 6 to 26 feet. (The height depends upon the tide.) Photographs showing the construction of the locks and some of the unusual vessels that have passed through are on display in the Administration Building. You can also take a self-guided walking tour of the Carl S. English Jr. Botanical Garden, seven acres of indigenous and exotic plants from around the world. Trout, salmon, and steelhead can be seen climbing the fish ladders from an underwater viewing window.

Opposite page: Seattle at night from Rizal Park

Totem pole and Pioneer Square Building

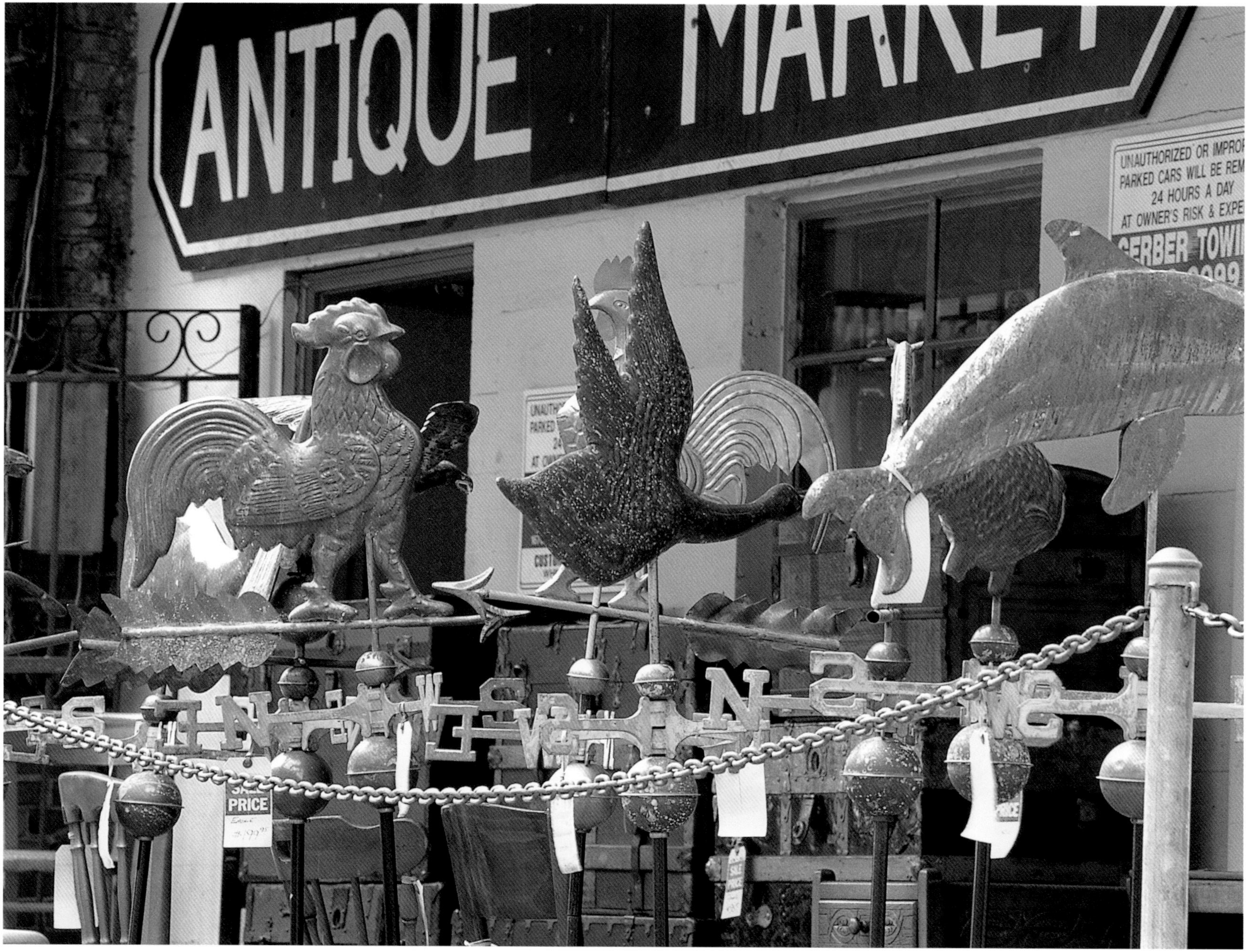

Antique Market

Neighborhoods

The natural hills and water boundaries of Seattle produce a rich mix of vibrant, intriguing neighborhoods that feel like small towns. Each has its own charm, whether it's classic or quirky.

Despite the early dreams of the city's leaders, Capitol Hill never received the honor of becoming Washington's capital. But no other neighborhood has a more vibrant sidewalk scene, day or night, than its main street. Along Broadway, there are movie theaters, clubs, taverns, private and community colleges, and probably one of the largest concentrations of Thai restaurants outside of Bangkok. By following the instructions of the bronze feet embedded in the sidewalk, you'll soon be dancing the waltz, tango, or two-step.

Capitol Hill also has one of the most diverse populations of any other neighborhood in Seattle. The gay community, grunge rockers, youth of many races, and longtime residents co-exist in harmony in historic mansions, elegant old homes, and remodeled apartment houses.

Despite its nearness to downtown, Queen Anne somehow retains its friendly, small-town character. Victorian mansions and cottages dating to the turn of the 20th Century grace the steep hillsides. Tiny shops and boutiques are popular with tourists and locals alike. Restaurants attract Sonics and Thunderbirds fans after the games with American, Italian, Thai, and French cuisine. The Standard Bakery makes some of the best cakes and pastries in the city. Sweeping views of the Space Needle, skyscrapers, Mount Rainier, and the endless marine traffic on Elliott Bay are at every turn in Queen Anne and its westward neighbors, Magnolia and Ballard.

Seattle's proud Scandinavian heritage runs deep in Ballard. The downtown area has brick streets, restaurants that serve lutefisk and AquaVit, shops selling crafts, and taverns where fishermen share seafaring yarns. The Alaskan fishing fleet winters at Fishermen's Terminal before embarking on its still-perilous quest. A 30-foot bronze memorial in the harborfront plaza commemorates the lives of those lost at sea.

For a closer look at the Scandinavians' contributions to the culture of the Pacific Northwest, stop by the Nordic Heritage Museum near downtown Ballard. Large galleries display a re-created immigrant settlement, handicrafts, and art.

Fremont, known by its free-thinking inhabitants as "The Center of the Universe," is Seattle's funkiest neighborhood. Highlights include the world's only public sculpture of a troll under a bridge devouring a Volkswagen, a sculpture of people "Waiting for the Interurban," a statue of Lenin, two microbreweries, and a Sunday market which doubles as a drive-in movie theater. Films are projected on the wall of a building painted white. Purple curtains, drawn and tied, are also painted on the wall to frame the projected image. I enjoy spending a rainy winter day in Archie McPhees browsing through bizarre, cheap items that make great party favors, the perfect gift for friends and family members with a sense of humor, or conversation pieces for the office. Whether you need rubber chickens or rubber checks from Ricochet Savings and Loan, you'll find it here. I've even found some of those old childhood favorites, such as Pez dispensers complete with refills, Super Balls, and miniature plastic dogs, cats, and dinosaurs in a variety of colors.

Wallingford is a comfortable neighborhood where the bungalows reflect its working class origins. Forty-fifth Avenue includes a Dick's Drive-In, another Seattle institution where generations of teens have congregated for their own "American Graffiti" experience. The thoroughfare continues east into the University District, where it is known simply as "The Ave." A mixture of inexpensive shops and cafés attract students from the University of Washington. On the northwest corner of the campus, the Burke Museum displays Northwest Coast artifacts, fossils, gems, minerals, and dinosaurs. The Henry Art Gallery,

Public Market Center at night

Post Alley at Pike Street Market

across Red Square from the Suzzalo Library, is the oldest public art museum in the state. Changing exhibits of historical and contemporary art is the museum's focus. Husky Stadium on the northern shore of Lake Washington is by far the most picturesque setting for watching Pac-10 college football. Many of the 72,500 fans arrive by yacht or sailboat and host lavish pre-game parties. Tail gate parties are also common in the stadium's parking lot. At the Museum of History and Industry in McCurdy Park, photographs and artifacts trace the growth of Seattle from a frontier settlement to a lumbering and shipbuilding center.

Wallingford and the University District are also linked by the Burke-Gilman Trail. Bikers and runners crowd the paved pathway, which continues 15 miles east into Bothell and beyond Woodinville.

The neighborhoods of Madison Park, Washington Park, Denny Blaine, Madrona, Leschi, Mount Baker, and Lakewood/Seward Park are a mix of upscale and middle-class residential areas along Lake Washington's western shore that often seem to blend together with majestic maples and firs, switchback streets, and homes perched on hillsides.

The Central Area in South Seattle has long been the heart of the city's African American community. A large Asian population lives here, too. In the 1930s, the area gained a national reputation for its up-and-coming jazz and blues musicians who played in its clubs and lived in its modest homes. Ray Charles, Quincy Jones, Jimi Hendrix, and Ernestine Anderson are just a few of the well-known artists who have lived here.

West Seattle is probably second to Fremont for its independent thinking. Recently, its citizens tried to annex from Seattle, but the initiative was quickly rejected by the Washington State Legislature. Despite swift growth resulting from its closeness to downtown, residents have managed to preserve the neighborhood's natural beauty and most of its historical buildings. Many of the homes perched atop the forested bluff overlooking the sound date back to the early 1900s. The Admiral Theater – closed for several years while locals fought to save it – has been restored and is open again, showing $2 movies in roomy, comfortable surroundings.

An assortment of fine restaurants line the south side of Harbor Avenue SW and are perched atop the bluff behind Alki Beach: Salty's, Pegasus, Spud's Fish and Chips, The Point, and Angelina's. At the West Seattle Junction, tiny shops sell antiques, clothing, candy, gourmet cooking supplies, compact discs, computer software, and greeting cards. Ten distinctive hand-painted wall murals recalling West Seattle's history and commemorating some of its major accomplishments are scattered throughout this business area. Scenes range from a streetcar chugging along California Avenue to the old wooden bridge connecting West Seattle to downtown.

Port of Seattle, Kingdome and city skyline

Moonrise over Seattle

Parks

Seattle's parks are as varied as the attractions downtown. In fact, three of the most unusual parks are in that area. Freeway Park, a plaza built on an overpass in commemoration of the Bicentennial, connects First Hill with the Washington State Convention Center and downtown's shopping district. The five acres are filled with rare evergreen bushes and trees, along with azaleas, marigolds, petunias, rhododendrons, and zinnias. Waterfalls and the Naramore Fountain muffle the constant traffic on the eight lanes of Interstate 5 below.

A few blocks away, Westlake Park (a brick expanse in front of Westlake Center between Fourth and Fifth Avenues), has become a popular gathering place for artists and street performers, ranging from a Jamaican band to dancing string puppets, and groups who support and oppose various causes. Benches attract office workers on their lunch hour and tourists interested in watching the crowds. The waterfall facing Fourth Avenue has a central walkway where you can walk through it without getting wet.

Harbor Steps, between Pike Place Market and Pioneer Square, is the newest park in the downtown area. This grand stairway descends First Avenue to the Waterfront. A series of waterfalls and plants invite people to relax and enjoy the panoramic view of the sound and mountains. In the foreground, a green and yellow electric-powered trolley cruises the tracks in front of the piers and docks.

Volunteer Park, one of Seattle's oldest parks perched high atop Capitol Hill, has something to do regardless of the weather. At the Asian Art Museum, one of the seven top collections of Asian art in the United States, you can peruse more than 2,500 Chinese paintings, sculptures, calligraphy, jade and bronze work, textiles, lacquers, and ceramics in six galleries. Japanese art, including a 17th century gold screen, fills six more galleries. Korean, Indian, and Southeast Asian art are also well represented. Nearby, the Conservatory is packed with cacti, orchids, and subtropical plants. If you're at the park on a clear day, climb the spiral staircase to the top of the 75-foot Water Tower for a 360-degree view of the metro area.

The Washington Park Arboretum near the University of Washington, called simply "the Arboretum" by locals, is considered one of the most beautiful floral, tree, and shrub displays in the Northwest. The drive or walk through the 200 acres is a treat in any season. In the spring, blossoms from rhododendrons, azaleas, magnolias, heather, mountain laurel, and dogwood grace the landscape. The shade of the red maples greets summer visitors on a warm day. When fall arrives, the leaves turn from green to red, orange, and gold.

Also inside the Arboretum is the Japanese Garden, 3.5 acres of miniature forests, mountains, bridges crossing trickling streams, tranquil ponds, ferns, mosses, flowering shrubs, a tea house, and an *azumaya* (resting place). Demonstrations of the Chado, an ancient tea ceremony, are offered the third Saturday of each month.

Another Japanese garden – one of my favorite escapes – is Kubota Garden in South Seattle. As soon as I'm strolling along the trails of these lush grounds, it's easy to forget a booming metropolis of more than a million people surrounds me. This serene 20 acres consists of gently sloping hills and pleasant valleys crisscrossed by streams, waterfalls, ponds, and rock outcroppings.

In the Central Area, a grass-roots campaign turned a vacant hillside into a 4-acre memorial to slain civil rights leader Martin Luther King, Jr. The centerpiece of the park is a 30-foot sculpture faced with Zimbabwe Black African granite in a reflecting pool. The tiles in the sculpture describe important events during the Civil Rights Movement, bear quotes from some of King's inspiring speeches, and display the names of the memorial's contributors.

Schmitz Park in West Seattle has one of the last remaining old-growth stands of timber in the city. A stroll through these 50.4 acres is like taking a short easy

Chief Seattle statue near Seattle Center

Totem pole in McCurdy Park

Sunset at Portage Bay, West Montlake Park

hike in the lower North Cascades. Approximately 2.5 miles of trails wind past Douglas fir and western red cedar, some over 140 years old. Many of these trees are so tall that you must stretch your neck and strain your eyes to see the highest branches. Skunk cabbages, swordferns, thimbleberries, Oregon grapes, and evergreen and red huckleberries form dense ground cover. Nurselogs support fungi, salal, and Douglas fir seedlings, while rushing creeks and birds add background music to your surroundings.

Sweeping panoramas from four city parks are the main attraction. In West Seattle, the view stretches from the Space Needle to Harbor Island at Belvedere and Hamilton View Points. Interstate 5 and Puget Sound form the crusts of a sandwich filled with skyscrapers from the vantage point at Jose Rizal Park on Beacon Hill. Perspectives change at Kerry Park on Queen Anne Hill, where skyscrapers cluster behind the Space Needle and Mount Rainier peeks out from behind the clouds on a clear day.

Woodland Park Zoo, across Aurora Avenue from Green Lake, has more than 1,000 animals and reptiles, most of which can be seen in exhibits that closely resemble their natural habitat. The 92-acre zoological gardens is a world leader in liberating animals from their cages and allowing them to roam free in natural settings. Habitats include the African Savanna, Northern Trail, Tropical Asia, Tropical Rain Forest, and an elephant habitat similar to Thailand. Evening outdoor concerts featuring folk, jazz, and classical music are held in the North Meadow in July and August. Zoo Doo is so popular among gardeners that the zoo sells the well-composted fertilizer by appointment only twice a year.

Unlike most major metropolitan areas, wildlife thrives inside Seattle's city limits. In the spring at Carkeek Park in the Broadview area, young chum salmon hatch in Venema Creek, which runs through the middle of the 223-acre park. Deer, coyotes, and 31 species of birds, ranging from rock doves to orange-crowned warblers, can be spotted along 13 miles of trails winding through dense forests, meadows, and a beach with sweeping views of Puget Sound and the Olympics.

Woodland Park Rose Garden

The famous neon coffee cup at Pike Place Market

*Klondike Gold Rush National Historic Center,
Pioneer Square*

Point Robinson Lighthouse (1885)

George Washington Bridge over Lake Union

Beautiful Suzallo Library at University of Washington

University of Washington Huskie Stadium and Lake Washington

Opposite page: Hiram M. Chittenden Locks

Ferry Issaquah loading at Fauntleroy dock at dusk

Ferry on Elliott Bay with Olympic Mountains backdrop

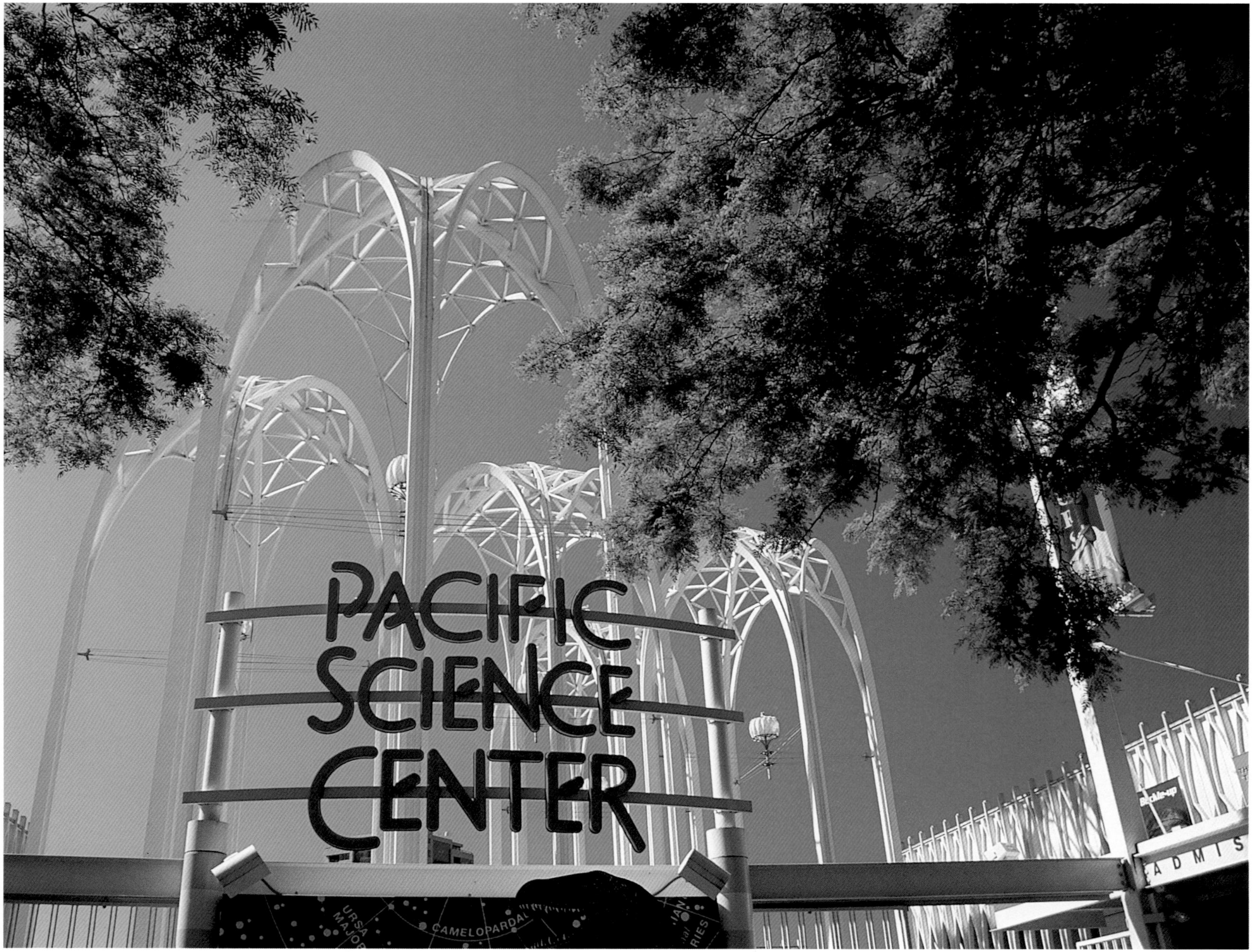

Pacific Science Center

Lake Union floating homes

Opposite page: Houseboats on Lake Union

The Montlake Bridge over Portage Cut

The Lacey V. Morrow Floating Bridge (I-90) crossing Lake Washington

The deep wooded ravines, forests, grassy meadows, and beaches at Discovery Park in the Magnolia neighborhood are home to more than 250 species of birds, including a pair of bald eagles. From May through early July, the eagles feed their chicks in a nest atop a tall bald fir at the north end of the 534-acre park. Remember your binoculars to get a close-up look. Free nature tours are offered every Saturday. The Sacred Circle Indian Art Gallery inside the Daybreak Star Indian Cultural Center has an impressive collection of contemporary American Indian art. On the beach behind West Point, archaeologists have excavated a 4,000-year-old Indian shell dump site, the oldest evidence of humans living in the Seattle area.

Cedar waxwings, raccoons, squirrels, chipmunks, screech owls, crows, beavers, cottontail rabbits, coyotes, foxes, deer, and beavers reside at Camp Long in West Seattle. Stroll the half-mile nature loop through the camp's 68-acre Douglas fir and western red cedar forest or join a free naturalist-led tour on the first and third Saturdays of the month. If you'd like to spend more time there, rent one of the 10 cabins available Tuesday through Saturday. A two-night minimum stay is required, and reservations must be booked two weeks in advance.

Sea lions, seals, and gray and Orca whales are often spotted from Lincoln Park, also in West Seattle next to the Fauntleroy Ferry Terminal. Two miles of trails wind through 130 acres of alder, hemlock, madrona, maple, western red cedar, and Douglas fir and descend 100 feet to Stony Beach at the western edge of the park. Some cedars and firs are as tall or taller than the bluff. Walk another mile along the U-shaped pebble beach or sit on a bench and watch the ferries glide across Puget Sound on the way to Vashon Island and Southworth on the Olympic Peninsula. If you're there early in the morning, chances are you'll see a bald eagle or great blue heron fishing from shore. Dress warmly if you hike the north end of Stony Beach, because cold breezes blow there year-round. The bluff protects the south end of the beach. The park also has tennis courts, horseshoe pitching courts, playground equipment, a wading pool, and an outdoor swimming pool.

Seward Park is another prime birdwatching spot. Dozens of species, ranging from California Valley quail to song sparrows, are visible along the 2.5-mile paved trail around the fish hook shaped peninsula. Park naturalists lead free nature tours on the second Saturday of the month.

In downtown Seattle, a pair of peregrine falcons has created a rare wildlife viewing opportunity at the Washington Mutual Tower on Third Avenue (between Seneca and University Streets). Here the raptors chose a ledge near the top of the skyscraper for their nesting site – a wooden box filled with gravel. From April through mid-June, the adults feed and teach the youngsters to fly. Washington Mutual Savings and Loan, the owner of the skyscraper, keeps a video monitor in the bank's lobby throughout the spring for the public to watch the chicks' progress. The Falcon Research Group tracks the raptors' movements to ensure the endangered chicks and their parents survive.

Plaza and trellis at the International District Metro Station

Opposite page: Mukilteo Lighthouse on Elliott Point

Out-of-Town Trips

Very few places in the United States offer the diverse range of out-of-town activities as the area around Seattle. Within an hour, you can take winery tours, eat Sunday brunch next to Snoqualmie Falls, hike alpine trails in the Olympics and Cascades in the summer, or ski at Stevens Pass, Snoqualmie Pass, or Crystal Mountain in the winter. Longer trips lead to the beaches of the Washington Coast, theme towns like the Bavarian village of Leavenworth and the Old West community of Winthrop, Lake Chelan, the fruit orchards in the middle of the state, and the deserts, forests, and wheat fields farther east.

Blake Island, between West Seattle and the Olympic Peninsula, remains virtually undisturbed. Other than Tillicum Village, the marina, three campgrounds, and 16 miles of hiking trails, the 475-acre island has probably changed little since the days when the Suquamish Indians used it as a camping ground. No ferries dock here while crossing Puget Sound, nor do bridges connect the island with Seattle proper or the Olympic Peninsula. The only way to get here is by tour boat or your own watercraft.

Deer, some 100 head, outnumber the handful of permanent residents employed by Tillicum Village. Mink, chipmunks, bald eagles, owls, and woodpeckers live in dense forests carpeted with ferns and meadows sprinkled with tiny baby blue and white wildflowers.

At Tillicum Village, Native Americans serve a traditional Northwest potlatch dinner of salad, hot bread, steamed potatoes, and freshly-baked salmon. The salmon is secured vertically to 5-foot cedar stakes and baked whole over an open alder pit fire. The skin remains on the body away from the fire to seal in the moisture.

As the guests dine in the longhouse, Native Americans dancers dressed in traditional costume tell stories of the struggle between good and evil. Before they perform each dance, a storyteller describes the legends that inspired each dance and then drums the beat that keeps the dancers in step with each other.

One of the dances I enjoyed the most was the "Taming Dance." According to the legend, an Indian brave traveled far away to a village north of his home. When he arrived, he was befriended by one of the village's residents, an evil spirit that managed to overpower the brave. When the brave returned to his village, he began saying unkind words to his friends and family.

The tribe met and created this dance, which chased the evil spirit from the brave and their village. It is performed by two dancers wearing bird head masks with 6-foot-long beaks. At intervals throughout the dance, they open and close the beaks, making a loud cracking noise that drives away the evil spirit.

After the performance, the guests can watch a resident Indian carver create traditional masks and totem poles, which are sold at the gift shop. Next to his display, they can watch a video of the British Columbia Indians filmed in 1913. The video includes a battle fought in canoes, a brave's stunning rescue of his kidnapped squaw, and some of the traditional dances performed with and without masks.

A number of quaint towns on the Olympic Peninsula make nice day trips. A 55-minute ferry ride across Puget Sound ends at Bremerton, the home of the Puget Sound Naval Base and the Puget Sound Naval Shipyard. Tour the naval museum and the *USS Turner Joy*, which fought in the Gulf of Tonkin incident in 1964.

Farther north, Poulsbo remembers its Norwegian heritage with Vikingfest in May, Skandia Midsommarfest in June, and the Yule Log Festival in November. Tiny gingerbread shops on the main street sell Norwegian crafts and food, including furniture, knick-knacks, afghans, and posters explaining the meaning of "Uff Da." Sluy's Bakery bakes lefsa, a potato pancake resembling a tortilla, pastries, and bread.

Port Townsend probably has the largest concentration of restored historical

Mount Rainier and Tahlequah ferry dock at dawn

Beautiful fall color at Quartermaster Harbor, Vashon Island

buildings of any other town in Washington. Structures built as early as the 1870's flank Water Street, the main street which runs along the waterfront, and Washington Street, one block north of Water Street. Most contain gift shops, antique stores, art galleries, and restaurants serving fare ranging from burritos to fresh seafood.

The Uptown District has dozens of century-old Victorian homes and churches which have been lovingly restored. Many are privately owned, while others have been converted into beds and breakfasts and lofts for writers and artists. Owners open their homes to the curious during self-guided historical home tours in May and September.

A pipe organ, one of the few remaining instruments made by Whalley & Genung in Oakland, California, is still played during services at the First Presbyterian Church, the first stone church built north of the Columbia River in 1887. The organ has 692 pipes and is the oldest in its original home in the state of Washington.

The Jefferson County Historical Museum and Maritime Library, formerly the City Hall, houses collections of early Victorian memorabilia and Indian artifacts and houses the genealogical society. The old jail in the basement is also open for tours. More than 50 species of birds have been identified in the wetlands, grasslands, and woodlands of Kah Tai Lagoon Nature Park. Fort Worden State Park contains officers' homes, barracks, a theater, parade grounds, and artillery bunkers dating from the turn of the century, when Fort Worden was a part of the harbor defense system for Puget Sound. Other highlights at the park include abandoned gun encampments, the U.S. Government Cemetery, Point Wilson Lighthouse, the Commanding Officer's Quarters, and the Marine Science Center. The Centrum Foundation hosts workshops and concerts throughout the year.

Sequim is known as the "blue hole" of the peninsula. Hidden in the shadow of the Olympia Mountains, it receives less than 20 inches of rain a year. Twice as much rain falls on Port Angeles, 24 miles west.

Just outside Sequim's city limits, you can take a driving tour of the Olympic Game Farm, a 90-acre preserve for animals used in wildlife films and television commercials. Bozo, the grizzly bear who co-starred in the popular television series, "Grizzly Adams," and the movie, "The Life and Times of Grizzly Adams," was trained here. Two roads circle through large fields of deer, guanaco, elk, bison, zebra, beaver, mouflon sheep, and a variety of birds. Predatory animals, such as lions, wolves, and tigers, are housed in a central compound at the center of the farm.

Seals are often spotted in the Strait of Juan de Fuca along the 5-mile walk of Dungeness Spit. At the end of the spit, volunteers give tours of the New Dungeness Lighthouse and maintain the grounds.

Beyond Port Angeles lies the Olympic National Park with 600 miles of alpine trails, lakes, rain forests, and wilderness beaches. My favorite stops in the park are Hurricane Ridge, Lake Crescent, and the Hoh Rain Forest. The untamed Ruby Beach, with its sea arches and offshore islands, is popular with avid hikers, and Sol Duc Hot Springs attract campers who want to soak in the natural mineral water.

More alpine trails can be found in Mount Rainier, Mount Saint Helens, and the North Cascades National Parks. The North Cascades are also a popular cross-country skiing area in the winter, and the City Light tour of its hydroelectric project on Diablo Lake is a treat in the summer. The tour includes a ride up an incline railway, another ride across the lake, a look inside the powerhouse at Ross Dam, and a country meal of fried chicken, mashed potatoes, and homemade apple pie.

Sun Lakes State Park is truly an oasis in the central Washington desert. This scenic 25-mile-long string of lakes along U.S. Highway 97 is a family-oriented place for those who enjoy hiking, fishing, trail riding, water skiing, swimming, picnicking, exploring geologic oddities, or simply relaxing in the sun.

Canada is literally in Seattle's backyard. Ride the Victoria Clipper to Victoria,

Salmon Bay Fishermen's Terminal

Opposite page: The City on the water, houseboats on Lake Union

British Columbia, and sample the city's British charm. Take high tea at the Empress hotel, complete with strawberries and cream, petit fours, and buttered bread with the crusts trimmed. Stroll through tidy gardens, shop at quaint shops, walk along the sea walls, visit Chinatown, and if Parliament isn't in session, take a free tour of the Parliament Building for a look at the beautiful stained glass windows and murals inside the dome. At the end of the day, you can catch another ferry back to Seattle or stay the night at one of dozens of hotels and bed and breakfasts.

"The Emerald City" is a place of opposites with moods that appeal to everyone: energetic yet relaxed, funky but conventional, cosmopolitan in the midst of some of the nation's most beautiful scenery. It's a young city with an Old West character. That pioneering spirit, clearly shown through the many innovators who were born or live here, is as strong today as when the Denny party landed at Alki in that dreary winter of 1851. If those early founders are still watching from somewhere – which I believe they are – they would be proud of what they have accomplished.

About the Author

Cheryl Landes is a freelance writer who has lived in the Pacific Northwest since 1977. More than 100 of her travel and history articles have been published in U.S. and Canadian magazines, including *Sunset, Northwest Travel, Oregon Coast, Adventure West, Rock and Gem,* and *Old West.* She is also a technical writer, editor, and indexer for a variety of corporations, ranging from computer software to transportation.

About the Photographer

Terry Donnelly, our feature photographer, is one half of a dynamite husband/wife photography team. He and his wife, Mary Liz Austin live on Vashon Island in the heart of Puget Sound in Washington. Together, they make one of the northwest's most prolific photographer combos.

Over the past 12 years they have traveled extensively in North American national parks, public and wilderness lands, popular tourist destinations and the scenic countryside in general. They seek out and capture those elusive vistas which reveal the mystery and grandeur of nature.

With his Washington base, Terry naturally spends time photographing his city of Seattle. Thus he was the perfect candidate for our new *Beautiful America's Seattle* book. One look through this publication and you will see why his images appear in numerous calendars, books, and projects by Sierra Club, Audubon, National Geographic, and *Outside* magazine.

Enjoy! You will be seeing more of his work.

Alpenglow on awesome Mount Rainier

Rear Cover: The Japanese Gardens